Descriptosaurus Punctuation in Action Years 4–6: Jack and the Crystal Fang

The only cure for a deadly plague sweeping the country is the crystal fang of a dragon that has terrorised the surrounding countryside for many years. Until now, the location of its den on Dragon Ridge Mountain has remained a mystery. In a race against time, Jack battles through a storm to reach the top of Dragon Ridge Mountain. With Merlin to guide him, Jack enters the dragon's den and comes face to face with the monstrous beast. This is a story of courage, magic and one boy's brave quest to fulfil a destiny foretold by the legends of long ago.

Join Jack on his journey as he writes the story with the assistance of Merlin the magician and Punctua (the Fairy Godmother of Writing), to punctuate properly and become a bestselling author.

Descriptosaurus Punctuation in Action Years 4–6: Jack and the Crystal Fang is part of a short series of age-specific, beautifully illustrated stories that can be read for pleasure and/or used as a contextualised resource, containing a step-by-step guide to teaching punctuation. The characters from each story are used to demonstrate a range of punctuation rules in a fun and engaging way appropriate to the book's age group. Areas covered include:

- ★ formulating punctuation rules.
- ★ the use of misconceptions to highlight common errors.
- ★ teaching tips to provide a punctuation model.

The book explores the impact of punctuation on reading, understanding, meaning and effect, and can be used as a basis for pupils' own punctuation or included in their 'Writer's Toolkit.' These new *Descriptosaurus* stories are an indispensable teaching aid for making punctuation fun for all primary teachers and literacy coordinators.

Alison Wilcox is the author of the *Descriptosaurus* series and has worked as a primary school teacher for many years. Whilst teaching, she developed *Descriptosaurus* to scaffold and improve children's creative writing, with dramatic results, and she made the decision to give up full-time teaching to work on the *Descriptosaurus* series. To keep up to date with current practices in schools, Alison undertakes brief teaching assignments, works with schools to develop new resources and conducts workshops for schools and teaching alliances.

Descriptosaurus Punctuation in Action Years 4–6

Jack and the Crystal Fang

Alison Wilcox

Routledge
Taylor & Francis Group
LONDON AND NEW YORK

First published 2022
by Routledge
2 Park Square, Milton Park, Abingdon, Oxon OX14 4RN

and by Routledge
605 Third Avenue, New York, NY 10158

Routledge is an imprint of the Taylor & Francis Group, an informa business

British Library Cataloguing-in-Publication Data
A catalogue record for this book is available from the British Library

Library of Congress Cataloging-in-Publication Data
Names: Wilcox, Alison, author.
Title: Descriptosaurus punctuation in action years 4-6 : Jack and the crystal fang / Alison Wilcox.
Description: Abingdon, Oxon ; New York, NY : Routledge, 2021. |
Identifiers: LCCN 2021008197 | ISBN 9781032040936 (hardback) | ISBN 9781032040950 (paperback) | ISBN 9781003190509 (ebook)
Subjects: LCSH: English language--Punctuation--Juvenile literature.
Classification: LCC PE1450 .W47 2021 | DDC 428.2/3--dc23
LC record available at https://lccn.loc.gov/2021008197

ISBN: 978-1-032-04093-6 (hbk)
ISBN: 978-1-032-04095-0 (pbk)
ISBN: 978-1-003-19050-9 (ebk)

DOI: 10.4324/9781003190509

Typeset in MyridPro
by Deanta Global Publishing Services, Chennai, India

Contents

Part C: Learning punctuation with the characters, level 2   117

Appendix   153

Dedication and acknowledgement

I would like to dedicate this book to all those wonderful teachers I have met and worked with who, despite any curriculum or assessment limitations, remain committed to finding creative ways of teaching.

Thanks as always to my family for all their support and encouragement, and for being patient and understanding when I "disappear into my fictional worlds." A special thanks to my son, Robert, for reading, reviewing and making some excellent suggestions as to how the story could be improved.

Thanks to Adam Bushnell. When you share a real joy of teaching and learning and get a fizz in the stomach when you see pupils getting excited about writing, you know you've chosen the right person with whom to collaborate.

Over 12 years ago, Bruce Roberts of Routledge took a chance on me as an author and *Descriptosaurus* as a concept. I am still indebted to him for his belief, encouragement and wise guidance.

Thanks to Molly Selby of Routledge for keeping us on track. Your support and efficiency are invaluable to completing the projects.

Huge thanks to the amazing and talented illustrators Nigel Clifton and Dani Pasteau for their contribution to this book.

Introduction

Research has demonstrated the negative impact SPAG (spelling, punctuation and grammar) has had on creativity. It has also revealed that the knowledge and application required in the context of the test have not resulted in a marked improvement in the quality of pupils' written texts as it is decontextualised and places emphasis primarily on identification and labelling. It does not, therefore, equip young writers to apply their knowledge of punctuation in their own writing, or, more specifically, assist them in developing a system for editing their own texts. In response, the new Ofsted Framework has focused on being able to demonstrate pupil progress in the writing process, which includes pupils being able to revise and edit their own written work.

Resources are, therefore, required to demonstrate, model and support pupils with understanding the editing process, as well as developing their knowledge of writing conventions. In addition to providing models in the context of a short story, there is a need for young writers to be able to investigate, discuss and explore texts to assess the impact of punctuation on the reading and understanding of a text.

Whilst most punctuation resources provide models, it is a useful exercise for pupils to be presented with incorrect punctuation so that they can begin to understand the importance of communicating a clear meaning and can use that knowledge and understanding when editing their own texts. Each of the punctuation sections in these short stories will examine rules, misconceptions and common errors as well as providing punctuation models.

The *Descriptosaurus: Punctuation in Action* series are companion books to *Descriptosaurus Story Writing: Language in Action*, which was designed to combine the need to develop descriptive vocabulary for a wide range of settings and characters with models of story and sentence structure, and grammar, as well as exercises to scaffold pupils as they innovate and invent their own models. There are four stories in the series: *The Ninjabread Girl*, *Captain Moody and His Pirate Crew*, *Ruby Red* and *Jack and the Crystal Fang*. Each story has been written in a different style and with the curriculum needs of each year group in mind. The individual stories can be used, innovated and deconstructed according to the level, experience and knowledge of each age group, class or individual.

The story of *Jack and the Crystal Fang* can be used for "reading for pleasure," but also contains a section on punctuation. The aim is to demonstrate punctuation in the context of a story and with characters that will have become familiar from reading the story. The characters are used to demonstrate a range of punctuation rules appropriate to the targeted age group:

1. formulating punctuation rules
2. using misconceptions to highlight common errors
3. using teaching tips to provide a punctuation model

They can be used as a basis for pupils' own punctuation posters and cards or copied to include in their 'Writer's Toolkit.'

JACK AND THE CRYSTAL FANG

Part A: The story of Jack and the Crystal Fang

The only cure for a deadly plague sweeping the country is the crystal fang of a dragon that has terrorised the countryside for many years. Until now, the location of its den on Dragon Ridge Mountain has remained a mystery. In a race against time, Jack battles through a storm to reach the top of Dragon Ridge Mountain. With Merlin to guide him, Jack enters the dragon's den and comes face to face with the monstrous beast. Will Jack defeat the dragon and rescue his village? This is a story of courage, magic and one boy's quest to fulfil a destiny foretold by the legends of long ago.

Part B: Learning punctuation with the characters

Jack wrote about his quest to find the crystal fang, which became a bestseller, but a few years later, he was faced with another equally challenging quest: an uprising by the apprentice writers across the length and breadth of Storyland. This became known as the Great Storywriting Rebellion.

Join Jack, Merlin and Punctua (the Fairy Godmother of Writing) as they tackle the rulers of Storyland, seek to overcome the rebellion with their Punctuation in Action campaign and get the apprentice writers to return to their desks and start writing again.

The three characters will take you on an editing journey through a series of punctuation Editing Quests divided into two levels. At the end of each level is a checklist for the writing apprentice to complete, together with two challenges: a punctuation editing challenge and a writing challenge.

In each level, Jack, Merlin and Punctua guide the apprentice to acquire the necessary knowledge, systems and skills to be able to tackle editing in their own writing and provide handy models for their 'Writers' Toolkit.'

Part A
The story of Jack and the Crystal Fang

1

The legend

DOI: 10.4324/9781003190509-1

Long, long ago, a terrible plague spread throughout the land. In towns and villages, people locked themselves in their homes. Crops rotted in the fields. All work had stopped. Every village had fever and sickness.

According to an ancient legend, the only cure was a powder made from the crystal fang of a dragon. This dragon was known to have its den in a cave in the north of the country and was known as *The Great Dragon of the North*.

King Arthur sent his knights to the north to search for the dragon's den. They searched and searched far and wide, but no one ever found the entrance.

One day, Merlin, King Arthur's most famous wizard, returned from the mysterious valleys of South Wales. Merlin knew the location of the dragon's den, but he also knew that it could only be entered by a special boy born with a silver mark on his right hand.

Eight years before, Merlin had taken this boy, who was called Jack, to live with a family in a village in the north until the time came when his powers were needed. Over the years, Merlin had visited Jack often and had watched him grow into a caring, hard-working young boy.

As the plague had spread through the land, Merlin had visited Jack and told him of the quest that awaited him. He had instructed him that on the sixth day of the new moon, Jack was to climb to the top of Dragon Ridge and Merlin would meet him there.

That is where our tale begins.

2

Dragon Ridge Mountain

DOI: 10.4324/9781003190509-2

It was early morning, and the top of the mountain was lit by brilliant, golden sunshine. Jack squinted into the sun and looked for the path to the dragon's cave. He could see the icy summit and the jagged, deadly peaks like daggers. A bubbling stream tumbled down the mountain. He stared at the steep rocky slopes, but he could not see the entrance to the dragon's cave. It was hard to find the path because the bottom of the slope was covered in mist like a white fleecy blanket.

Jack's heart dropped. "How am I going to find the path now?" he thought anxiously. "How am I going to rescue the village?" Jack groaned and slumped against a boulder.

Suddenly, Jack heard a voice roar in his head. "Use the beans."

Jack had forgotten about the beans in his pouch. He didn't know how they could help, but he had no other plan. Jack put his hand in the pouch around his waist. The beans felt warm and hairy and a disgusting cheesy smell rose from the pouch. He quickly threw the beans on the ground.

Immediately, an odd tingling trickled through his body. When Jack looked up the mist had parted. Now, he could clearly see a narrow, winding path up the side of the mountain. The beans were magic!

He could see things far, far away. He could see the smallest rock and tiny creatures. Then, he spotted the entrance to the dragon's cave hidden behind three big, black boulders.

Jack closed his eyes. Instantly, he could see the inside of the cave. Enormous skeletons covered the floor of the cave. He could not see or hear the dragon, but he could smell smoke, burning flesh and rotten eggs.

When he opened his eyes, Jack's stomach lurched. "Oh no!" he gasped. Huge, dark clouds raced towards the mountain. "I can't turn back now," thought Jack, gritting his teeth.

Somewhere above him, Jack heard Merlin shout, "Get moving now."

Jack knew there was no time to lose, so he started to climb.

3

The storm

DOI: 10.4324/9781003190509-3

Jack stepped onto the path and into a tunnel of swirling, cold mist. It was like a giant creature was sending its huge icy breaths down from the top of the mountain. The mist floated above his head, curled around his body and slithered over his feet.

Hour after hour, Jack trudged on and on. Slowly, he climbed and scrambled his way towards the icy summit. He crawled along narrow ledges and clambered over big black boulders like giant marbles scattered across the path. Finally, Jack thought he was getting closer to the top because he could feel the air getting colder.

Although Jack knew his climb was coming to an end, he was getting tired and his legs were aching. He didn't think he could climb much further, but the thought of his parents urged him on. "Not far now. Keeping going, Jack," he kept muttering to himself.

But Jack's luck had run out. The storm had arrived: first, a rumble of thunder in the distance and then the whistle of the wind around the mountain. Before long, the thunder crashed and howled over his head. The wind whined and shrieked as it tore the mist into ragged sheets. Huge boiling black clouds raced towards the mountain.

The wind shoved and tugged fiercely at Jack and he struggled to stay on his feet. It made it impossible to walk. Jack was sure he would be blown off the path. "Where are you, Merlin? Help me!" Jack yelled.

The thunder roared louder. Then, lightning like a flashing spear lit up the path. Next came the rain. It hammered on his back and stung his face. It was as if he were being blasted by a fire hose, and Jack was soaked from head to foot. It was hard to breathe. It was hard to walk, and Jack wasn't sure he would make it, but he kept on climbing.

Suddenly, a loud crack made Jack jump out of his skin. He looked up and froze. An enormous, dazzling arrow of lightning lit up the sky. It ripped through the clouds and struck the path in front of him. Jack pressed his back against the side of the mountain and held his breath as a giant crack appeared at his feet. There was nowhere to go. He was trapped. "Merlin! Help me!" Jack sobbed as the ledge disappeared and he tumbled through the air into the dark void below.

4

Merlin

DOI: 10.4324/9781003190509-4

Jack spun wildly head over heels through the air. It felt as if his ears were going to burst. His eyes were bulging out of their sockets. Jack braced himself for the impact with the ground. But it never came.

One moment he was tumbling through the air towards the ground and the next Jack felt a fleecy pillow slide underneath him. When he opened his eyes, he saw that he was surrounded by what looked like a giant ball of cotton wool. All around him was brilliant white. He was in the middle of a cloud, and it was drifting slowly beneath him.

Suddenly, the movement stopped. The bottom of the cloud slid open like a trap door and deposited Jack on the ground. When he looked up, the cloud had vanished like a puff of smoke.

Jack looked around. He was at the entrance to the dragon's cave and Merlin was waiting for him.

"I thought I was too late." Merlin's voice boomed out across the mountain.

"I d … d … didn't th … think I was g … g … going to make it," Jack stammered. He could barely speak. His teeth were chattering and his whole body was shaking. The cold and dampness from his sodden clothes had seeped into his bones and was making him shiver uncontrollably.

Jack squeezed out the sleeve of his wet tunic and looked up at Merlin towering above him. His long white hair and beard blew in the wind. Merlin really was a terrifying figure.

"You ch … ch … chose the wr … wrong b … b … b … boy, ssssir," Jack stammered. "I ammm nnnot b … brave. I … am n … n … not s … str … strong. I … I … I am not cl … clever."

Merlin leaned towards Jack and put an arm around his shoulder. He pointed at the silver mark on Jack's right hand. "This is how I know, Jack, that you are the boy the legends speak of." Merlin raised his huge bronze staff and moved it slowly around Jack. A hot wind gusted around Jack's legs, then his body and finally his arms and head. Jack's clothes were soon dry.

"You need to get your strength back before you face the dragon," Merlin said, guiding Jack towards a boulder and sitting down beside him. Merlin put his hand inside his long, woollen cloak and pulled out a wooden tankard. He handed it to Jack. The smell of cinnamon and honey wafted up Jack's nose. It was bubbling and it warmed his hands.

"Come on, down in one. You'll feel better once you have something warm inside you," Merlin said kindly.

Slowly, Jack lifted the tankard to his dry lips and took a tiny sip. A delicious, sweet taste flooded his mouth. Jack was very thirsty and drunk it down in one gulp. Energy raced through his body like an electric current. "Thank you, Merlin," Jack said, handing the tankard back to the wizard.

"Do you feel better now?" Merlin asked. Jack nodded. "Good. We haven't got long. We need to move fast. Listen carefully. The roast duck I left for the dragon has gone, so it should be asleep soon. But the sleeping potion I sprinkled on it is a new recipe and I'm not sure how long it will last."

"Crows' claws! Do you mean the dragon might wake up while I'm trying to get its fang?" Jack said, his eyes wide with fear. "I can't do this!" he said, shaking his head.

Merlin stared at him a moment and then pulled out a pink stone dangling from a leather thread. He leant over and hung it around Jack's neck. "Wear this. It will protect and guide you. It is you, Jack, and you alone that can rid this land of the plague. In every family, every house, every village there is sickness, fever and death. With the dragon fang, you will create a kingdom free of disease and sickness. We are all relying on you, Jack."

Jack took a deep breath. "But what do I do if it discovers me before the sleeping potion works? How do I extract the crystal fang? What do I do if it wakes up?"

"So many questions," Merlin chuckled. "Never fear, Jack. I will be there to guide you."

"If you are with me, I will try," Jack said quietly.

Merlin nodded. "When you enter the cave, you will see a tunnel ahead of you. Follow this tunnel until you come to a second cave where there is an enormous pit in the centre. But stay away from the pit. This is where you will find the dragon." Merlin paused to make sure Jack understood his instructions.

Jack nodded.

"If the dragon finds you before the sleeping potion has worked, stand still and look it in the eye. Hold the crystal in your right hand. It will light up the mark on your hand. Whatever you do, do not look away."

"What will happen if I look away?" Jack whispered.

"You will no longer be protected," Merlin replied. Jack nodded. His heart was racing at the thought of staring into the eyes of a dragon.

Merlin dug inside his cloak and pulled out a leather bundle. Carefully, he unwrapped the leather parcel to reveal a purple paste. "Wait until the dragon is asleep, then rub this paste onto its gums."

Jack leant over to look at the paste but quickly raised his head. It stunk of beetles, bats and bitter berries.

Merlin smiled. "It doesn't smell good, but it will work. The fang will drop out quickly, so make sure you have your hands ready to catch it. Then wrap it carefully in the leather pouch."

"Aren't you coming with me?" Jack asked.

"No, Jack. I cannot enter the cave, but that stone is my eyes and ears. I will be able to guide you through the stone and I will be waiting for you when you return." Merlin closed the leather parcel and handed it to Jack, who slid it into the pouch around his waist.

Suddenly, Merlin stood up and beckoned for Jack to follow him. "It's time, Jack."

5

The portal

DOI: 10.4324/9781003190509-5

"Stand in front of the centre boulder," Merlin told Jack.

Jack glanced to his right and watched as Merlin first grasped his golden staff in both hands and then raised it above his head. In a voice that echoed around the mountain, he said: "Through the power of all that is good, I ask you to show this boy the way."

Jack could not take his eyes off the bright light glowing from the end of the staff. A sudden gust of wind whirled around Merlin, sending his cloak flapping like giant wings around him.

When the wind had died down, Merlin lowered the staff onto the centre boulder. He closed his eyes and slowly rocked backwards and forwards. It was as if he was in a trance as he chanted over and over again, "Dangos y ffordd inni; dangos y ffordd inni; dangos y ffordd inni."

Jack was frozen to the spot as he watched the boulder sizzle. Soon a crack appeared. It was just big enough for a small boy to squeeze through.

Merlin turned to Jack and said: "When you pass through the boulder, you will come to a wall of rock. Look carefully and you will see the pattern of a hand carved into the rock. Place your right hand here and the door will open."

A rush of cold air swirled around Jack. He glanced to his right. Merlin had vanished. Jack's heart thudded in his chest. He was on his own!

Jack felt for the stone around his neck and heard Merlin whispering in his head, "Remember all that I have told you. Quick, before the opening closes."

He glanced back one more time and then slid through the gap in the boulder.

Immediately, Jack spotted the hand carved into the rock, so he stepped towards the wall and placed his hand over the rock. A strange prickling sensation shot through his fingers and his palms. Soon, a streak of flashing light shot from each of his fingers and spread out like a shimmering rainbow across the wall. Before long, it began to ripple, and an arched doorway appeared.

Above the doorway was a giant white stone arch. A shiver charged down Jack's back. On top of the archway was painted an enormous dragon, and its massive wings stretched across the whole arch.

"There isn't much time, Jack," Merlin's voice whispered in his head.

Jack took a deep breath and, without looking back, walked through the door.

6

The cave

DOI: 10.4324/9781003190509-6

Jack had entered an enormous cave. He stopped at the entrance and took in his surroundings. It was icy cold and turned his breath into misty clouds. Jack's heart pounded in his chest. He saw huge skeletons, skulls and bony limbs scattered across the ground. Above him, stalactites like giant fangs hung from the ceiling. Water trickled down their sides and collected in smooth, shiny pools of ice at the bottom. Across the centre of the cave, huge columns of twisting stone erupted from the floor. Strange writing and symbols covered them from top to bottom.

Jack scanned the walls of the cave looking for the tunnel. Suddenly, he spotted it in the right-hand corner at the back of the cave and started to walk towards it. He had taken no more than a few steps when the light vanished. He spun around and his insides twisted with terror. The door had vanished. He was trapped. Not for the first time he wondered why he had agreed to this quest.

When he looked across the cave, Jack could only see shimmering shadows and the shapes of the rocky columns rising out of the gloom.

Jack felt for the stone around his neck. He felt a buzzing in his palm and fingers like an electrical current pulsing through his veins. Suddenly, it made him feel brave and strong enough to conquer anything and now he could hear Merlin whispering. "Use your hands and feet to feel your way."

It took a moment for Jack's eyes to adjust to the dark. He tried to picture the layout of the cave. To cross the cave to the tunnel, he would have to wind his way between the forest of rocky columns and pray there were no traps he had not spotted. Then, he remembered the pools of ice at the base of the stalactites. Although time was running out, Jack knew he would have to inch his way carefully across the cave.

Slowly, Jack moved across the cave, waving his hands in front of him and sliding his feet cautiously one by one across the floor. With every step, the bones cracked and shattered like dry, dead branches under his feet. Every few steps Jack stopped and listened, but all he could hear was the drip, drip, drip of the water. No sign that the dragon had heard him.

Jack made painfully slow progress. He hadn't gone far but had already scratched his knuckles on the stone columns and bumped his head on the stalactites. Twice, he had stumbled over a bone or rock and crashed to the floor, scraping his hands and knees. "This is useless. I'll never get to the tunnel," he said.

A breeze brushed against his face like a cold, thin strip of air and he heard Merlin whispering, "Let the breeze be your guide, Jack."

By keeping the breeze in his face, Jack was able to move more quickly across the cave and it was not long before he saw it. A flame flickering in front of him. "It has to lead to the dragon's den," Jack thought. "Now, at least I have some light to guide me."

The flickering flame grew brighter and brighter, so Jack knew he had to be near the tunnel. And then, the breeze disappeared and was replaced by steaming gusts of hot air. Jack froze and listened for any sound. His eyes darted right and left, trying to pierce the darkness, searching for the slightest movement. Nothing. It was still quiet. He could feel the sweat running down his neck and back. The steaming air was filled with a revolting stench of sulphur and rotten eggs.

Before long, Jack entered a high, circular cavern. In the centre of the cave was an enormous pit. He could hear it bubbling and boiling like tomato soup. He saw it spitting bright red jets of flame and clouds of steam into the air.

The sound of cracking, crushing and crunching echoed around the cave. Jack shrunk back against the wall and held his breath. He watched and waited.

7

The dragon

DOI: 10.4324/9781003190509-7

All of a sudden, the crunching stopped, and it was silent. The only thing Jack could hear was his heart pounding in his ears. Seconds later, the silence was broken by the swish, swish, swish of a tail across the ground. *"Oh no! It knows I'm here."* Jack's legs trembled and it took a mighty effort not to run.

A whoosh of stinking air struck Jack in the chest and pinned him against the wall. Sweat dripped down Jack's forehead and into his eyes, but he dared not raise his arm to wipe it away.

The stone throbbed against his chest and Merlin's warning echoed in his head, "Stand still. Do not move."

A deafening boom shook the ground, then another and another. The dragon was coming towards him. Jack could hear its talons clicking on the stone floor. He could smell its stinking breath. His heart hammered in his chest. Still, Jack didn't move.

Slowly, Jack raised his right hand towards the stone. When he looked up, the enormous red dragon was towering over him. Its head was bigger than a boulder and it had scales like sharpened steel spikes. Its long tail whipped from side to side.

A sick feeling gurgled in the pit of Jack's stomach. He held his breath as it lowered its head. Its huge emerald green eyes stared at Jack's hand. Jack glanced down. The silver mark was glowing.

The dragon bent closer until its nostrils were nearly touching Jack's face. Still, Jack did not move but kept looking into its green eyes. He gripped the stone tighter until he could feel it pressing into his palm and forced himself not to look away.

Jack felt that at any moment his legs would buckle under him and he would be the *dragon dessert*. But without warning, the dragon's head suddenly slumped onto its chest and its huge jaw dropped open. Its enormous forked tongue hung out and it dribbled giant strands of slime from the corner of its mouth. Its eyes rolled in its head and then, with an almighty groan, it crashed to the floor. Jack dived to the side just in time.

For what seemed like hours, Jack stood against the wall watching the dragon. "Now, Jack," Merlin whispered.

Slowly, Jack moved towards the dragon and knelt down at its head. He slid the leather bundle carefully out of his pouch and unfolded it. He was terrified that at any moment it would wake up, so he kept glancing up at the dragon. He could see that it was asleep because its chest gently rose and fell in a steady rhythm.

Jack took a deep breath to block out the stinking stench from the purple paste and stuck his fingers into the putrid slime. He eased the dragon's jaw open wider so he could see the fang. Immediately, he spotted it like a gigantic crystal dew-drop sparkling at him.

Jack had to push through huge strands of dragon drool and his hand soon became slimy and slippery. He had to grit his teeth to stop his stomach heaving. He was glad he hadn't had anything to eat because he was sure he was going to be sick.

Eventually, Jack felt the glassy fang. As quickly as he could, Jack smeared the paste along the gums and sat back.

Within seconds, there was a sizzle and a crack. Quickly, Jack pushed his hand into the dragon's mouth and waited for the fang to drop out. One side of the fang slid out of the gum and dangled down into the dragon's mouth. Jack put his hands under the fang and waited for the other side to drop. Seconds later, it slid into Jack's hands.

It was hard to hold onto the fang because it was covered in slime and slobber and kept slipping out of Jack's hands. With a sigh of relief, Jack wrapped the fang in the strip of leather and carefully placed it in his pouch.

He was just rising to leave when he realised that it had gone quiet. Quickly, he glanced at the dragon. Its chest was still moving up and down. But a prickle spread across Jack's neck. The dragon's eye had flickered briefly. It could be awake any minute. Had he taken too long?

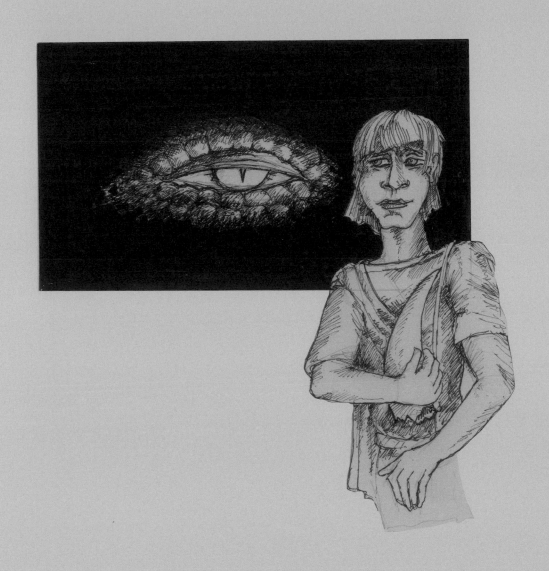

8

The escape

DOI: 10.4324/9781003190509-8

As quick as he could, Jack headed towards the tunnel. He was nearly at the end of the passage when he felt the ground tremble under him. The walls shook and the tunnel echoed with the piercing screech of the dragon. Suddenly, Jack felt a scorching heat on his back. When he spun round, he saw a column of fire tearing down the tunnel towards him. Frantically, he flattened himself against the wall and pressed his palms to his ears to block out the high-pitched shrieks.

The stone throbbed and Jack slid his hand around it. He watched in amazement as the flames burst towards him and then arched away centimetres from covering him in a blanket of fire. Instead, the flames struck the opposite wall and tore down the tunnel.

Jack ran, his arms and legs pumping as he belted down the tunnel. He could see a narrow beam of bright light ahead of him and sprinted towards it. He dodged the rocky columns and ducked under the giant stalactites. All the time, he could hear the dragon's thunderous footsteps and its roar somewhere behind him. Finally, he saw the door in front of him and headed towards it.

He was halfway across the cave when a spear of swirling fire exploded into the cave. It shot towards the ceiling and one after another the stalactites collapsed and crashed to the floor. One shattered at his feet. Jack staggered backwards and tripped over a rock. He fell onto his arm and a terrible pain shot through his body.

For a moment, Jack felt dizzy and sick and he couldn't move. He sat on the ground and hugged his arm to his chest. All around him, rock rained from the ceiling. The thudding was getting nearer and nearer. The ground under him was trembling.

"Get up, Jack. Get up, *now*!" Merlin roared in his head.

Slowly, Jack eased himself up and started to move. A pain shot through his knee and for a moment Jack's leg buckled under him. Jack gritted his teeth and staggered as fast as he could towards the door. Dazzling sunlight blinded him for a moment. When Jack glanced round the door had disappeared. All he could hear was the piercing roar of the dragon.

Jack's legs finally gave way and he crashed to the ground. Two ox-hide sandals appeared in front of him and Jack looked up into the beaming face of Merlin. "Well done, Jack. Only 'The Healer' could have got that fang from the dragon. It is your destiny to be the most powerful wizard for good in this land."

Jack returned to his village a hero. The powder from the dragon's fang saved his parents and his village, and rid the country of the killer plague. Over the years, Jack travelled the land healing the sick and destroying the plagues that threatened his country.

9
The Great Story-Writing Rebellion

JACK

My home, Storyland, is a place where time as you know it doesn't exist and stories are valuable treasures. It is a place of magical creatures, dangerous animals, knights and quests, battles and plagues. Everyone was happy in Storyland until one day there arose the Great Story-Writing Rebellion; all storytelling suddenly stopped.

PUNCTUA

In every story ever told, my sisters, the other Fairy Godmothers, have been heroines. My eldest sister was a box office hit at the Meeting House with the story of her adventures with Cinderella. Imagine then, what it felt like for me to be the first fairy godmother in the history of Storyland (and that's a long, long time) to be a *villain*! During the days of the Great Story-Writing Rebellion, I was even called a "devilish fiend"! Young children chanted, "Punctua shun" when I passed. I was

DOI: 10.4324/9781003190509-9

someone to be avoided or even rejected. I was misunderstood and abused.

One day, I went with Jack to the Land of Schools (it was not a good trip for either of us). I discovered that the rulers in the Land of Schools had started punishing their young for not using my punctuation. They were beaten with wooden sticks, detained in classrooms and made to rewrite their stories over and over again; it was hardly surprising that I had become a villain in Storyland.

No matter how much I told them, they would not listen when I tried to convince them that I was a hero who helped young writers. Using my punctuation system, my "Punctua's Points," their writing would become clear and anyone that read it could understand their story, were no longer confused and enjoyed reading it.

Well, thanks to the rulers of the Land of Schools, the young storytellers had got the wrong message and had stopped writing stories. And I can't say I blamed them. Writing stories had become a list of rules, red pens and punishments. No longer was there any excitement about writing – the apprentice writers went on strike.

JACK

The campaign:

Punctua and I decided that we needed a campaign to break the deadlock in the Story-Writing Rebellion. We needed to find a way of speaking directly with the apprentice writers and persuade them that punctuation wasn't bad, took time to learn and master, but should never stop them from writing their stories. We needed to find a platform to publicise my journey to becoming a famous author.

I set up a social media site called *The Trumpeter*, and quickly attracted lots of followers. Below are the appeals we posted on the site. Within a short space of time, word had spread and Punctua and I had lots of requests to visit schools and the apprentice writers.

@TheTrumpeter.storyland
#all-young-apprentice-writers
#end-the-story-writing-rebellion

The Great Story-Writing Rebellion is causing poverty and famine for many families in Storyland. As they no longer have stories to sell, they cannot pay their taxes. Instead, crops and animals are being taken by the vile Sheriff and his tax collector.

Please abandon the Story-Writing Rebellion and return to Storyland. It is truly a magical place where imagination is *king* and Punctua is a fairy godmother and not an evil witch.

Without Punctua's help, I could never have written the story of my quest for the Crystal Fang. Using her punctuation system, my writing made sense to my readers, and I was able to write the story in a way that made it an exciting, vivid adventure that became a bestseller and sold millions of copies all over the world. I have even been approached by a number of film studios, who are keen to turn the story into a film. Please do not "shun" punctuation. It will take time to learn, understand and master, but that will only happen if you pick up your pens and start writing again. Learning about punctuation should not be just about learning but using the system to improve a story you have written to make it even better.

Jack (www.JackandtheCrystalFang.com)

@TheTrumpeter.storyland
#all-young-apprentice-writers
#end-the-story-writing-rebellion
#Punctua-fairy-godmother-not-villain

I beg you not to think of me as a villain. I really am the hero of Storyland. I am always here to help you tell your wonderful stories. I am not here to punish you, but to show you how to use my punctuation to make sure your readers can read and understand your stories. I am pleading with you to pick up your pens once again, end the Story-Writing Rebellion and make me the Godmother of Writing once more. Punctua {.,?! ";:-}(x)

@TheTrumpeter.storyland
#rulers-officials-knights-Land-of-Schools
#end-the-story-writing-rebellion
#Punctua-fairy-godmother-not-villain

Our story is not only for young apprentice writers; it is a guide for you in your battle against the Story-Writing Rebellion. Throughout my time with Jack and during our many quests and challenges, I have endured many crises. On a number of occasions, I have had to take a period of rest and recuperation in the Land of Holydays. A few years ago, I spent some time in rehab during the Incident of the Internet Malfunction and the Menace of the Messages. There, I was able to gain some insight and perspective, and am now fully recovered and back in Storyland.

Eventually, I came to understand that the purpose of my punctuation system varies according to whether it is standard or non-standard writing. For many years I didn't understand why my messages to my Fairy Godmother sisters had upset and even angered them. During a family meeting, I came to realise that although the lack of a full stop was a messenger menace to me, to others, including a full stop made them think I was upset or angry.

Now, I am much calmer and whenever I have a relapse, I remind myself that writing is "communication." It is not just how I write it that is important, it is the way my communication is understood.

You will have your own crises, battles and challenges, but I hope as you tackle the quests that Jack and I had to face, you and your young writers will use punctuation as a tool to help you make their writing clearer, easier to read and more exciting. I hope that young apprentice writers are now safe from the consequences of not obeying "rules," that they will be encouraged to tell their stories once again and that we can finally bring to an end the Story-Writing Rebellion. Good luck.

(Knights in the Land of Schools are called teachers and parents).

THE BOOK

Punctua and I wrote this book to tell the story of how I managed to transform my first draft of the *Jack and the Crystal Fang* into a bestseller. It is an account of how Punctua taught me punctuation rules and how to use them to edit my work. I hope it inspires you to write. But remember, you can always call on Punctua and the knights in the Land of Schools if you need help turning your first draft into a masterpiece.

The book is divided into three parts:

1. The story of *Jack and the Crystal Fang*
2. Quests level 1
3. Quests level 2

The quests are divided into two levels because some of the quests, challenges and battles in level 2 may be unsuitable for younger or less experienced writers. It is essential that you have been fully trained, have acquired all the necessary skills and are confident in the basic techniques in level 1 before you move on to level 2.

At the end of level 1, there is a checklist that needs to be completed before you can have access to level 2.

There is also an Appendix where you will find examples of how to use bullet points:

★ an advert
★ a mission statement

I have also included a copy of the Wanted Poster displayed in all the surrounding villages when I first disappeared on my quest.

Merlin insisted on including his prologue, but he has taken out some punctuation and mixed up others to set you a final challenge for when you have completed levels 1 and 2.

FINAL NOTE

Thanks to the campaign and success of this book, even though it took some time, we did manage to bring an end to the Story-Writing Rebellion.

Although we have ended the Great Story-Writing Rebellion in Storyland, news reaches us that the Rebellion is yet to be defeated in other lands and other times. Hopefully, our campaign will spread so that rulers in the western parts of the Land of Schools will stop testing and punishing their young writers and use our story as a beacon of hope for writers everywhere.

To encourage you to write, we have written an alternative version of Jack's journey to the top of Dragon Ridge Mountain where Jack is stranded in the tunnels inside the mountain. Your job is to give Jack a number of challenges, including some other dangerous creatures and obstacles he has to face, before he finally arrives at the top of the mountain and meets Merlin.

Jack and Punctua

Part B

Learning punctuation with the characters

10

Meet the characters

Section 1: Jack

Section 2: Merlin

Section 3: Punctua (the Fairy Godmother of Writing)

DOI: 10.4324/9781003190509-10

SECTION 1: JACK

To all apprentice writers who find writing and punctuation difficult. Take heart from this message.

I'm Jack, the author of this story. Once, I felt exactly as you do. When Merlin told me that I had to record my quests for the Legend Library, I kept making excuses as to why I didn't have time to write them. I didn't want to tell him that I found writing difficult because all the events got muddled up in my head. I was also particularly bad at punctuation. Even though Merlin made me write out his punctuation rules every day, and practise punctuating the sentences and paragraphs he wrote, when it came to editing my own writing, I still found it really difficult.

However, time ran out and I could no longer make any excuses. I sat down to write the stories, which was a daily torment, with Merlin standing over my shoulder scolding me for missing out some detail or being careless and sloppy about punctuation.

I hadn't got far when Punctua, the Fairy Godmother of Writing, paid me a visit. Without her patient guidance, this book would never have been finished, and I was so proud when it was published and reached number one in the Legend Library Charts. More importantly, now I understand what writing process suits me best, and how to edit my work, I love writing and have already started my new book.

I have great sympathy for your plight because of my own experiences, but it doesn't have to be like that. Writing is fun and rewarding. If I can master punctuation, so can all of you. Following the quests in this book will make the writing and editing process easier; punctuation will start to make sense; the rulers and knights will soon see the error of their ways just as Merlin did.

Jack

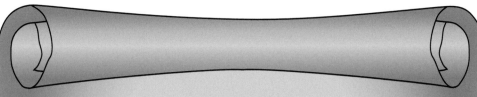

SECTION 2: MERLIN

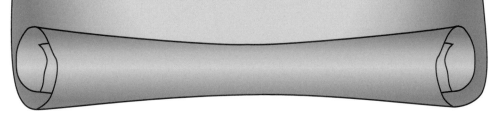

Well done, Jack. Your name may be on the front cover of the book, which is at number one in the Legend Library Charts, however, I think I deserve far more credit than I have been given. I did scold you, but that was because I thought you were being sloppy. I had no idea that despite all the hours I spent teaching you punctuation, and the numerous exercises I wrote for you, you still didn't know how to edit your own writing.

Reading the note from Punctua, I have to say that she has greatly exaggerated her part in the success of my Book of Spells, and there was never any chance that my spells would have turned anyone into a wart-covered spider.

On a final note, I have to admit that despite all your trials and tribulations, you are now a very accomplished writer, and your success should encourage all apprentice writers to get back to work.

Merlin

SECTION 3: PUNCTUA (THE FAIRY GODMOTHER OF WRITING)

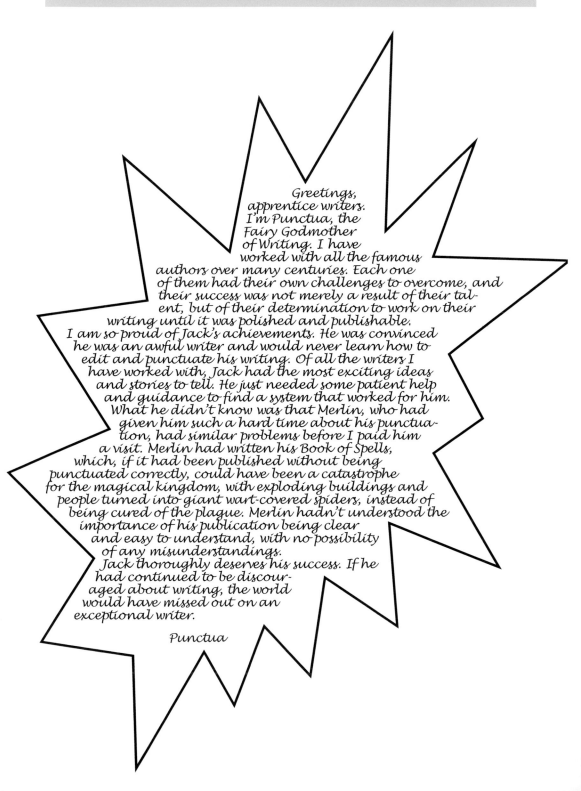

Greetings, apprentice writers. I'm Punctua, the Fairy Godmother of Writing. I have worked with all the famous authors over many centuries. Each one of them had their own challenges to overcome, and their success was not merely a result of their talent, but of their determination to work on their writing until it was polished and publishable.

I am so proud of Jack's achievements. He was convinced he was an awful writer and would never learn how to edit and punctuate his writing. Of all the writers I have worked with, Jack had the most exciting ideas and stories to tell. He just needed some patient help and guidance to find a system that worked for him.

What he didn't know was that Merlin, who had given him such a hard time about his punctuation, had similar problems before I paid him a visit. Merlin had written his Book of Spells, which, if it had been published without being punctuated correctly, could have been a catastrophe for the magical kingdom, with exploding buildings and people turned into giant wart-covered spiders, instead of being cured of the plague. Merlin hadn't understood the importance of his publication being clear and easy to understand, with no possibility of any misunderstandings.

Jack thoroughly deserves his success. If he had continued to be discouraged about writing, the world would have missed out on an exceptional writer.

Punctua

11

Editing a story

Quest 1:
Ending the period drought in the unit of sense

Section 1: Writing tips

Section 2: Editing a story

Section 3: Tackling the sentences

DOI: 10.4324/9781003190509-11

SECTION 1: WRITING TIPS

Editing a story

The process:
- ★ Write a story outline.
- ★ Split the story into scenes.
- ★ Read aloud and edit.
- ★ Check grammar, spelling and punctuation.

JACK'S WRITING TIPS:

When I started to write, I either just sat staring at the blank page and didn't know what to write, or it felt like my head was being "boiled." All the events got muddled in my head, so I missed out really important parts of the story.

Punctua showed me a system where I write a brief outline of the quest, and then break it down into scenes. I find it easier to get started by just writing some brief notes as a plan. This way, I also don't have to hold too many events in my head while I'm trying to write. It helps me to remember more of the important details.

Punctua helped me create punctuation cards I could refer to when I am editing my stories and showed me how much easier it is to spot your mistakes by reading the text aloud.

She used my story to teach me how to punctuate correctly and, suddenly, I could understand the mistakes Merlin had kept pointing out. Like magic, it all made sense.

Merlin had never really explained what a sentence is, and because I didn't understand this, none of the rest of the punctuation made sense. Once I understood the basics of a sentence, I could read my story aloud and hear where the sentence needed to end to ensure that my writing made sense and flowed. When I had mastered the basics, Punctua showed me some tricks and tips on how to use punctuation to change the pace of the story and create suspense and excitement.

Jack

PUNCTUA'S POINTS:

When you start writing your story:

★ write a brief outline of the plot.
★ divide the story into scenes.
★ add more events and details to the plan of each scene.

When you are editing your writing, **read it aloud** and:

★ note when you **pause.**
★ put a pencil mark at that point on your text.

Ask:

★ Why did I **pause**?
★ Was it because:

    a. the thought, statement, idea or description was **complete**?
    b. you had to re-read what was written because it **didn't make any sense**?

★ Could I:

    a. combine some of the sentences to improve the flow of the writing?
    b. shorten some of the sentences to increase suspense?

SECTION 2: EDITING A STORY

Editing a story

The first draft:

Read it aloud.

Does it make sense?

Check full stops and capital letters.

JACK'S FIRST DRAFT:

Jack squinted into the sun looked for the path to the dragons cave could see the icy summit and the jagged deadly peaks like daggers.

MERLIN'S MOANS:

Where are the full stops? It doesn't make any sense. I first read it as if the cave could see the icy summit. *Really*, Jack! How many times have I told you not to forget *full stops* and *capital letters*! Not to mention the missing apostrophe.

PUNCTUA'S POINTS:

To insert full stops and capital letters, Jack first needs to understand what a sentence is.

Punctuation is a series of traffic signals. Without it, words bang together, and your writing won't make any sense. It will take your reader a long time to get to the end and they could get terribly lost.

A **full stop** is the most important **punctuation mark**. It helps you to **signal to your reader** that the **sentence has ended**, and the statement (thought, description, idea) is **complete**.

When reading your first draft, ask yourself these questions:

1. Is this a sentence?
2. Does it make **sense**?
3. Is it **complete** or do extra words need to be added?
4. Does it start with a **capital letter** and end with a **full stop**?

In Jack's first draft, there were no full stops or capital letters, and no complete sentences.

Jack squinted into the sun looked for the path to the dragons cave could see the icy summit and the jagged deadly peaks like daggers.

1. We need a **capital letter** at the start – which Jack remembered.
2. Where is the first complete statement? Jack squinted into the sun.
3. Where is the second complete statement? He looked for the path to the dragon's cave.
4. Where is the third complete statement? He could see the icy summit and the jagged deadly peaks like daggers.

Note: Jack could have joined the first two statements with **and** to **combine them into one sentence**.

So, the first complete sentence could have been:

Jack squinted into the sun, and he looked for the path to the dragon's cave. *(cave belonged to the dragon = dragon's cave)*

There is a **capital letter** *at the start and a* **full stop** *at the end. The two sentences are* **joined** *together using* **and**.

SECTION 3: TACKLING THE SENTENCES

Sentences

There are four types of sentences:

★ Statement (.)
★ Question (?)
★ Command/instruction (.)
★ Exclamation (!)

JACK'S RULES:

He stared at the steep, rocky slopes. **(statement)**

I can't climb that! **(exclamation)**

How am I going to rescue the village? **(question)**

Use the beans. **(command)**

MERLIN'S MOANS:

It didn't seem to matter to Jack what type of sentence it was, *they all ended in a full stop*. I don't know how many times we have gone through exclamation marks and question marks. The beans were magic. Where are you, Merlin. (I despair!) Didn't I teach you anything?

PUNCTUA'S POINTS:

Remember: punctuation marks are a series of traffic signals.

Punctuation marks make it **easier to read** and **understand what has been written** and **how** it is meant to be **read** or **spoken**.

(There are more tips about question marks and exclamation marks later.)

It is true to say that **every sentence ends with a full stop**.

Look closely at the **bottom** of a **question mark** and an **exclamation mark**. What do you notice?

Both have a full stop at the bottom!

Example:

The beans were magic**!** (surprise)

Where are you, Merlin**?** (question)

Recap:

A **sentence** is a **unit of words** that is **complete** and **makes sense**.

It can be a **statement**, **question**, **exclamation** or **instruction**.

A **sentence** always **starts** with a **capital letter** and **ends** with a **full stop**.

12

Capital letters

Quest 2:
BaTtle oF ThE caPitaLS

Section 1: Beginning of every sentence and names of people

Section 2: Names of places

Section 3: Starting a sentence, 'I,' names of people, places, days of the week, months of the year, and titles of books, films, songs and television programmes.

Section 4: Editing checklist

DOI: 10.4324/9781003190509-12

SECTION 1: BEGINNING OF EVERY SENTENCE AND NAMES OF PEOPLE

Capital letters

★ start every sentence.
★ are used for names of people.

JACK'S RULES:

Capital letters are used:

★ to start a sentence.
★ for the names of people.
★ for 'I.'

Examples:

Jack heard **M**erlin shout, "Get moving, now."

MERLIN'S MOANS:

There is absolutely no excuse for forgetting capital letters for names, particularly Merlin. You've seen it written on my spellbook often enough.

Jack heard merlin shout get moving now.

Are you are referring to the bird, merlin, which is a species of falcon or *me*? I'm not even going to mention "quoting my words!"

PUNCTUA'S POINTS:

Capital letters are **signposts** that help us to understand a text, spot the **characters** and **places** easily.

Jack remembered to **start his sentence** with a capital letter.

However, he forgot about the **names of people**.

Merlin is the name of the wizard, and it should start with a capital letter.

The bird, merlin (a species of falcon) does not start with a capital letter. Your reader could have assumed that merlin was a "talking falcon."

SECTION 2: NAMES OF PLACES

Capital letters

★ start every sentence.

★ are used for names of people and 'I.'

★ are used for names of places.

JACK'S RULES:

Capital letters are used for:

★ names of **places**.

Examples:

One day, Merlin returned from the mysterious valleys of **S**outh **W**ales.

Jack was to climb to the top of **D**ragon **R**idge **M**ountain.

MERLIN'S MOANS:

Well, at least in your first draft you managed a capital letter for Wales.

Names, places, days and months start with a capital letter. Write that in your book and correct this sentence. What on earth is this?

Jack had to meet merlin, who had just returned from the valleys of south Wales, at the summit of dragon ridge mountain on the first sunday in march.

PUNCTUA'S POINTS:

Capital letters are **signposts** that help us to spot the **names of places** easily.

Jack remembered that **Wales** is the name of a **country** so it starts with a **capital letter**. However, he forgot that **South Wales** is the name of a region in **Wales**, so **South** should also have a capital letter.

Remember: if a **forest, river, mountain, town, village, city** or **region** (**North Yorkshire, Warwickshire**) have a name it starts with a capital letter.

He should have written:

Jack had to meet **Merlin**, who had just returned from the valleys of **S**outh **W**ales, at the summit of **D**ragon **R**idge **M**ountain on the first **S**unday in **M**arch.

SECTION 3: STARTING A SENTENCE, 'I,' NAMES OF PEOPLE, PLACES, DAYS OF THE WEEK, MONTHS OF THE YEAR, AND TITLES OF BOOKS, FILMS, SONGS AND TELEVISION PROGRAMMES

Capital letters

1. start every sentence.
2. are used for:
   - ★ names of people and 'I.'
   - ★ names of places.
   - ★ days of the week.
   - ★ months of the year.
   - ★ titles of books, films, TV programmes and songs.

JACK'S RULES:

Capital letters are important. They **start a sentence** and should be used for:

a. names of **people**, as well as '**I**.'
b. names of **places**.
c. **days** of the week.
d. **months** of the year.
e. **titles** of books, films, TV programmes and songs.

MERLIN'S MOANS:

What happens if you forget capitals, Jack? Mayhem, mystery, misunderstanding, that's what! Don't keep forgetting:

- ★ days of the week: Sunday, not sunday.
- ★ months of the year: March, not march; march is to stride like a soldier.
- ★ Jack and the crystal fang. This is the **title** of your story, isn't it?

PUNCTUA'S POINTS:

I gave this model to Jack to keep in his **Writer's Toolkit**. Whenever he can't remember when to use capital letters, he can use this **model** to help him. It's always useful to have a model to look at when you are editing.

My name is **Jack**. **I** live in a village at the foot of **Dragon Ridge Mountain**. **One Sunday**, in **March**, I set off for **Dragon Ridge Mountain** to meet **Merlin**, who had just returned from the valleys of **South Wales**. **I** wrote the story of my quest to rid the country of a deadly plague in my book, ***Jack and the Crystal Fang***, which has been turned into a film, ***The Quest for the Crystal Fang***. **A** song has also been written in my honour called "**Silver Hand**."

SECTION 4: EDITING CHECKLIST

Capital letters
1. start every sentence.
2. are used for:
   ★ names of people and 'I.'
   ★ names of places.
   ★ days of the week.
   ★ months of the year.
   ★ titles of books, films, TV programmes and songs.

EDITING CHECKLIST:

I found it hard to remember where to put capital letters, so Punctua and I came up with this checklist to use when I am editing.

I take each item one at a time:

1. beginning of every sentence ☐
2. names of people ☐
3. 'I.' ☐
4. names of places ☐
5. days of the week ☐
6. months of the year ☐
7. titles of books, films, TV
   programmes and songs ☐

13

Question marks

Quest 3:
Interrogation in the Centre of Questions

Section 1: Direct and indirect questions

DOI: 10.4324/9781003190509-13

SECTION 1: DIRECT AND INDIRECT QUESTIONS

Question marks

Question marks:

★ go at the end of direct questions.

Direct questions mean the exact words of the speaker are reported.

JACK'S RULES:

Question marks go **at the end** of **direct questions**, which usually begin with words like:

Who? What? When?

Why? Where? How?

Is? Are? Can? Will? Do? Did? Would? Could?

MERLIN'S MOANS:

What do you call someone who doesn't pay attention in his lessons?

Who said that he had checked his punctuation?

Why does he not listen to me, even though I am the greatest wizard of all time?

Is there any hope that Jack will ever finish this story?

Could he become a great writer in time?

PUNCTUA'S POINTS:

Young writers:

* ★ get **direct** and **indirect questions** confused.
* ★ forget the **question mark** at the **end of the sentence**.

Direct question (question mark at the end):

* ★ where the speaker's **exact words are repeated**

For example:

Do you feel better now**?** **Will** the dragon wake up**?** **When** did the dragon take the roast duck**?** **What** will happen if I look away from the dragon**?**

Indirect question (no question mark):

* ★ where the exact words are **not repeated**

For example:

Merlin **asked Jack** if he was feeling better. Jack **asked Merlin** what would happen if he looked away from the dragon.

14

Exclamation marks

Quest 4:

The quest for excitement at Shrieking Point

DOI: 10.4324/9781003190509-14

Exclamation marks

Exclamation marks are used to show:

★ surprise.
★ an outburst.
★ humour.

JACK'S RULES:

Exclamation marks signal:

★ **surprise**: Crows' claws!
★ **an outburst**: I can't do this!
★ **humour**: What happened to the naughty wizard at school? He was ex-spelled!

MERLIN'S MOANS:

In his first draft, Jack either forgot to signal a surprise or an outburst by using an exclamation mark, or he put exclamation marks at the end of every sentence, even though I told him not to over-use exclamation marks, which was really *irritating*!

Exclamation marks were once called *shrieks*. They need to be saved so that when they are used, the reader knows you are experiencing strong emotions, and are shocked or terrified. According to your first draft, you were shaking in your boots throughout the story. By the way, I never use exclamation marks for humour because I don't like jokes.

PUNCTUA'S POINTS:

Exclamation marks are a **signal** to the reader that the **character** has a **strong emotional reaction** to something.

It could be:

★ a **surprise**.
★ an **outburst**.
★ a **joke**.

Example:

Help me, Merlin**!**

Crows' claws**!** What do you mean you haven't used the potion before?

They are extremely useful for **emphasis** but should **not** be used **too often**.

15

Inverted commas

Quest 5:
The quest for Quotation, the "God of Speech"

Section 1: When and how to use inverted commas

Section 2: How to punctuate inside the inverted commas

DOI: 10.4324/9781003190509-15

SECTION 1: WHEN AND HOW TO USE INVERTED COMMAS

Inverted commas (speech marks)

Inverted commas: (speech marks) are used to:

★ identify dialogue (direct speech).

★ enclose the exact words spoken.

Use commas to separate speech from the rest of the sentence.

JACK'S RULES:

★ Use **speech marks** to **quote the exact words** someone has **said**.
★ Usually use **"double quotation marks"** (*66* and *99*).
★ Speech marks are also called **inverted commas**.

Example:

"Quick, before the opening closes," Merlin urged.

★ **the exact words spoken by Merlin**
★ enclosed within **speech marks** at the **beginning** and the **end**
★ a **comma** separates the words spoken and the speaker

MERLIN'S MOANS:

In the first draft, Jack wrote:

Get up, NOW Merlin roared in his head

I had difficulty working out what exactly you had said.

At first, I thought you meant that someone was telling me to get up.

PUNCTUA'S POINTS:

1. Get up, NOW Merlin roared in his head.

To ensure that the reader doesn't get confused about **who is talking** and **what they say**, we need to use **speech marks** to **separate the speaker** and **their words**.

"Get up, NOW!" (This is what Merlin said.)

To **separate the speech from the rest of the sentence** and make it clear **what is being said by whom** we **need** a **comma**.

"Get up, NOW," Merlin roared in his head.

(Note: the comma comes inside the speech marks.)

We could have put the **speech at the end**, but we still need a **comma** to **separate the speech** and the **speaker**.

Merlin roared in his head**,** "Get up, NOW."

SECTION 2: HOW TO PUNCTUATE INSIDE THE INVERTED COMMAS

Inverted commas (speech marks)

★ The words a person says always begin with a capital letter.

★ Question marks and exclamation marks go inside the speech marks.

★ If the quotation ends a sentence, put a full stop before the closing speech marks.

★ Start a new line for each new speaker.

JACK'S RULES:

1. The **words** a person **says** always **begin** with a **capital letter**.

For example:

"**S**tand in front of the boulder," Merlin said.
(Merlin said, "**S**tand in front of the boulder.")

2. The **question mark** or **exclamation mark** goes **inside the speech marks**.

For example:

"Help me**!**" Jack yelled. "Where are you, Merlin**?**"

3. If the **speech ends a sentence**, a **full stop** goes **before the closing speech marks**.

For example:

Merlin's voice boomed out across the mountain**,** "**I** thought I was too late**.**"

4. Start a **new line** every time there is a **change** in the **person speaking**.

MERLIN'S MOANS:

In the first draft, Jack wrote:

"The sleeping potion I sprinkled on the roast duck may not last long. Do you mean the dragon might wake up? Jack said.

I think you'll find I sprinkled the sleeping potion on the roast duck, and you were the one who was terrified of the dragon waking up, Jack.

PUNCTUA'S POINTS:

It can be very confusing for the reader if dialogue is not punctuated correctly.

Top tip:

> **Start** the speech using a **capital letter inside the opening speech marks**.

> **End** the speech with a **comma, full stop, question mark** or **exclamation mark inside the closing speech marks**.

Tricky bit:

When the quotation is **interrupted**, it can get a bit tricky. Look at the following examples:

> **"T**he sleeping potion I sprinkled on the roast duck is a new recipe and I'm not sure how long it will last**,"** Merlin said anxiously.

If we break this quotation up:

> "**T**he sleeping potion I sprinkled on the roast duck," Merlin said anxiously, "is a new recipe and I'm not sure how long it will last."

Note: break up the speech using: (i) a **comma after the first words spoken**, (ii) a **comma after the speaker** and (iii) **no capital letter when the speech is restarted**.

16

Apostrophes

Quest 6:
The search for the attachments of the apostrophes

Section 1: To show possession (discovering what belongs to whom)

Section 2: To show possession (discovering if it's one or more)

Quest 7:
The apostrophe myst'ry of the missing letters

Section 3: To show when two words have been joined together and some letters are missing

Section 4: Editing checklist

DOI: 10.4324/9781003190509-16

SECTION 1: TO SHOW POSSESSION (DISCOVERING WHAT BELONGS TO WHOM)

9 Apostrophes

Apostrophes are used to:

★ show possession (that something belongs to someone).

JACK'S RULES:

An apostrophe (') + s **shows possession**.

It shows that **something** is **owned** by **someone** or is **connected** to **something**.

For example:

The fang belonging to the dragon.

The dragon**'s** fang.

The golden staff belonging to Merlin.

Merlin**'s** golden staff.

MERLIN'S MOANS:

In the first draft Jack wrote:

The dragons' fang.

You knew an apostrophe had to go somewhere *but* you guessed because you didn't know *where*.

He also wrote:

Crops rotted in the fields'.

PUNCTUA'S POINTS:

1. Dragons' fang.

   There is only a **single** dragon. The **fang belongs** to **one dragon**.

   Who **owns** the **fang**? The **dragon**.

   Add **'s** to dragon = **dragon's** fang, *not* **dragons'** fang.

2. Crops rotted in the fields'.

   Does anything **belong** to the fields? **Not that we are told**. No need for an apostrophe.

   Crops rotted in the **fields**. (fields is plural)

SECTION 2: TO SHOW POSSESSION (DISCOVERING IF IT'S ONE OR MORE)

Apostrophes

★ Apostrophes are used to show possession.

★ For plural nouns ending in 's,' just add an apostrophe after the 's.'

JACK'S RULES:

If something is owned by more than one person and the plural noun ends in 's':

For example:

The claws belonging to the **crows**.

crow**s** ends in '**s**.'

Add an **apostrophe** after the 's.'

The **crows'** claws.

MERLIN'S MOANS:

In the first draft Jack wrote:

The caves's entrance was blocked by three huge boulders.

The skeletons's limbs were scattered all over the floor of the cave.

PUNCTUA'S POINTS:

The caves's entrance.

There is **more than one** cave.

The plural of cave is **caves**. It ends in '**s**.'

As it already ends in 's,' just **add an apostrophe after the 's.'**

★ **the caves' entrance**

Skeletons's limbs.

The limbs belonged to more than one skeleton.

The plural of skeleton is **skeletons**.

It already ends in 's,' so **add an apostrophe after the 's.'**

★ **skeletons' limbs**

What if the **plural** noun **doesn't end in 's**'?
For example, **children**.
You need to add **apostrophe and 's**': **children's stories**

JACK'S RULES:

If the something is owned by a **singular noun**, for example, **Thomas**, which ends in '**s**':

For example:

medicine belonging to Thomas

Thomas already ends in '**s**.'

Example:

Thomas' medicine

Apostrophes

★ Apostrophes are used to show possession.

★ For singular nouns ending in 's,' just add an apostrophe after the 's.'

MERLIN'S MOANS:

In the first draft Jack wrote:

Thoma's medicine.

Tiberiu's war.

More guesswork!

PUNCTUA'S POINTS:

Example: Thomas' medicine

The medicine belongs to **Thomas**.

Thomas is **singular** and **ends in** '**s**.'

Add an **apostrophe after** '**s**.'

Thomas' medicine

Example: Tiberius' war

The war belongs to Tiberius.

Tiberius is **singular** and **ends in** '**s**.'

Add an **apostrophe after** '**s**.'

Tiberius' war

SECTION 3: TO SHOW WHEN TWO WORDS HAVE BEEN JOINED TOGETHER AND SOME LETTERS ARE MISSING

Apostrophes: contractions

Apostrophes are used to show when:

★ two words have been joined together.

★ some letters are missing.

MISSING!

JACK'S RULES:

When **two words** have been **joined** and **shortened**, apostrophes are used to **replace the missing letters**.

For example:

I'm (I **am**); you're (you **are**); she's (she **is**); it's (it **is**);

they're (they **are**); he'll (he **will**); can't (can**not**); don't (do **not**); there's (there **is**)

MERLIN'S MOANS:

Thank goodness, Punctua helped Jack to edit his story before it went to the publIshers. Despite all the lessons I gave him, he got **it's/its, they're/their** and **you're/your** terribly mixed-up, so his writing didn't make any sense whatsoever.

He wrote:

Jack could hear **it's** talons clicking on the stone floor. (What is "it is talons"?)

In towns and villages, people locked themselves in **they're** homes. (What is "they are homes"?)

I give up! I don't know how many times I've explained this. Over to you, Punctua.

PUNCTUA'S POINTS:

Don't be unkind, Merlin. Many young writers make the same mistake as Jack. I seem to remember you had a few problems yourself.

When young writers are completing their first draft, initially they forget the apostrophes or mix them up. It is, therefore, important that they have a list of contractions in their Writers' Toolkit to use when they are editing.

Using the list, read through the draft and underline any of these words so that they can be checked for the correct punctuation.

Editing checklist – contractions:

I'm, you're, he's, she's, it's, we're, they're, there's, I'll, you'll, he'll, she'll, we'll, they'll, can't, didn't, don't, wont, couldn't, wouldn't

Many young writers mix up its/it's, their/they're and your/you're. They need to remember that words like his, her, **its, your** and **their** that show **possession do not** have an **apostrophe**. They are an exception.

SECTION 4: EDITING CHECKLIST

Apostrophes

Don't confuse:
★ it's/its
★ they're/their
★ you're/your

PUNCTUA'S POINTS:

★ its (belonging to **it**)
★ it's (it **is**)
★ their (belonging to **them**)
★ they're (they **are**)
★ your (belonging to **you**)
★ you're (you **are**)

Example 1:

Jack could hear **its talons** clicking on the stone floor. (**The talons belonging to it**.) ✓

Jack could hear **it's talons** clicking on the stone floor. (Jack could hear **it is** talons.) ☒

It's fangs glistened with slime and slobber. (**It is** fangs.) ☒

Its fangs glistened with slime and slobber. (**The fangs belonging to it**.) ✓

Example 2:

They're homes. (**They are** homes.) ☒

Their homes. (**The homes belonging to them**.) ✓

Example 3:

 You're recipe didn't work. (**You are** recipe.) ☒

Your recipe didn't work. (**The recipe belonging to you**.) ✓

Once he understood the difference between they're and their and its and it's, Jack edited his sentences to:

Jack could hear **its talons** clicking on the stone floor.

In towns and villages, people locked themselves in **their** homes.

Your recipe didn't work. The dragon woke up before I could leave the cave.

Editing checklist: apostrophes					
Contraction		*Contraction*		*Contraction*	
I'm	I am	There's	There is	Can't	Can not
You're	You are	I'll	I will	Won't	Will not
He's	He is	You'll	You will	Don't	Do not
She's	She is	He'll	He will	Didn't	Did not
It's	It is	She'll	She will	Couldn't	Could not
We're	We are	It'll	It will	Wouldn't	Would not
They're	They are	We'll	We will		

17

Commas
The comma maze

Quest 8:
The confusing, bemusing and baffling list comma mystery

Section 1: In a list

Quest 9:
Separated by the extras in the comma meaning break

Section 2: To avoid misunderstandings

Section 3: To separate parts of a sentence

Quest 10:
The, plague of, the comma, splicers

Section 4: Comma splicing

DOI: 10.4324/9781003190509-17

SECTION 1: IN A LIST

Commas

★ separate items in a list.
Use and to separate the last two items on a list.

JACK'S RULES:

Commas separate items in a list to make the meaning clear.

Instead of saying:

It stunk of blood **and** beetles **and** bats **and** bitter berries.

Replace **and** with a **comma**.

Use **and** to separate the last two items in the list.

It stunk of blood**,** beetles**,** bats **and** bitter berries.

MERLIN'S MOANS:

If you don't use **commas to separate items in a list**, it can be very confusing.

It stunk of blood beetles bats bitter berries.

This could be read in many different ways, which could be disastrous when making up a potion.

For example:

It stunk of blood beetles, bats bitter and berries.

PUNCTUA'S POINTS:

Commas are needed to make the meaning of a **list** clear and avoid any misunderstandings.

A comma can be used instead of **and**. It signals a slight **pause** between the **words or phrases** and helps the sentence to flow and not sound too jerky.

Use **and** to separate the **last two items** on a list.

The list should have been written:

It stunk of blood, beetles, bats, and bitter berries.

SECTION 2: TO AVOID MISUNDERSTANDINGS

Commas

★ identify the person/people being addressed.

★ make the sentence clearer and easier to read.

★ avoid any misunderstandings.

JACK'S RULES:

Commas are used to **separate the person/people** being identified **from the rest of the sentence**.

For example:

I will try, Merlin.
I will try Merlin.

MERLIN'S MOANS:

My brain rattled when I read what Jack had written in his first draft. Did he think I had committed a crime?

"I will try Merlin."

I thought what on earth is he going to try me for. I haven't committed any crimes.

PUNCTUA'S POINTS:

Commas are needed to make the meaning clear and avoid any terrible misunderstandings.

Jack needs to think carefully whether he is talking **to someone** or talking **about someone**.

Example:

"I will try Merlin." With **no comma to separate try from Merlin**, this means that Jack is talking **about trying Merlin**.

"I will try, Merlin." The **comma separates try from Merlin**, so Jack is **talking to Merlin** and saying that he will try.

Example:

"Drink Jack. You will feel better." With **no comma to separate drink from Jack**, Merlin is talking **about drinking Jack**.

"Drink, Jack. You will feel better." The **comma separates drink from Jack**, so Merlin is **telling Jack** to drink.

SECTION 3: TO SEPARATE PARTS OF A SENTENCE

Commas

★ separate parts of a sentence to help make the meaning clear.

★ add extra information to the main part of a sentence.

JACK'S RULES:

A comma is used to:

★ **separate parts of a sentence** to help make the meaning clear.

★ **add extra information** to the **main message** of a sentence.

1. When joining two complete sentences, commas go:

    Between the **first complete sentence** and the **conjunction** (and, but, so, or).

    Example:

    Jack threw the beans on the ground**, and** the mist suddenly disappeared.

2. When adding extra information to a complete sentence, commas go:

    Between the extra information and the main sentence.

3. The extra information often starts with conjunctions like:

    when, before, after, if, until, while, although

    Example:

    Before the mist disappeared**,** Jack had not been able to see the path up the mountain.

MERLIN'S MOANS:

It didn't seem to matter how much I explained the rules, I couldn't get Jack to understand. He wrote:

Merlin put his hand inside his cloak and he pulled out a wooden tankard.

Although he could not see the dragon pit he could smell the stench of sulphur.

PUNCTUA'S POINTS:

As young writers start to experiment with **longer, more complex sentences** and vary how they start their sentences, they often get confused about where to insert **commas** or forget them altogether.

Short, simple sentences are fine and can be useful when, for example, you are trying to build drama and suspense in a scene. *But*:

★ too many short, simple sentences can make the writing sound a bit jerky and prevent it flowing.
★ too many long, complex sentences can be confusing and ramble on and on.

Ideally, writers should use a mixture of both short simple sentences and longer complex sentences.

You can link your sentences and make them longer by:

a. **joining two complete sentences** together. For example, using conjunctions like **and**.
b. **adding extra information to** the **main part** of the sentence using conjunctions like **when**.

Adding **extra detail** or information to the main part of the sentence helps:

i.   to explain **why** something happened.
ii. to explain the **result** of something happening.
iii. to change the **time or place**.

a.   joining two sentences

Jack threw the beans on the ground. The mist suddenly disappeared.

These two complete sentences can be joined using **and**.

Jack threw the beans on the ground**, and** the mist suddenly disappeared.

Note: there is a **comma before and** to link the two sentences.

b.   adding extra information

The reason the mist disappeared was **because** Jack threw the beans on the ground. Jack could link the sentences by writing:

When Jack threw the beans on the ground**, the** mist suddenly disappeared.

This time, Jack is **not joining two complete sentences**. He is **adding some extra information** to the main message to make it clear why the mist disappeared.

Main message – The mist disappeared.

Extra information explaining why – When Jack threw the beans on the ground.

When he threw the beans on the ground doesn't make sense on its own. To make sense, it needs to be linked to the main message by a comma.

Note:

i.   the conjunction **when** at the beginning.
ii. the **comma after** the extra information.

Example:

Jack was exhausted**,** **but** he kept climbing. (joining two complete sentences)

Although Jack was exhausted**,** he kept climbing. (adding extra information to the main message for contrast and emphasis)

Tip: look out for the following **conjunctions** that help add more detail to your writing.

When, before, after, if, until, although

SECTION 4: COMMA SPLICING

JACK'S RULES

Sometimes two **sentences** link ideas, thoughts or descriptions and you want to join the sentences together.

A comma *cannot* be used to join two sentences. This is called **comma splicing**.

You need to use a **conjunction** to link the two sentences.

He could see inside the cave, **but** he couldn't see the dragon.

MERLIN'S MOANS:

This boy splices everywhere. I shout, "Splicing, Jack. You've done it again. Use a conjunction or end the sentence. I'm wasting my breath. *Fanboys*, Jack! *Fanboys*!"

Jack closed his eyes, instantly he could see the inside of the cave, enormous skeletons covered the floor of the cave he couldn't see the dragon.

PUNCTUA'S POINTS:

For your writing to flow and not sound jerky, it is important to **vary the length of your sentences**.

But **two complete sentences cannot be joined by a comma**.

You need to use a **conjunction**, for example: **and, but, so, for, yet, or**

When editing your writing, *check*:

★ how many complete statements are included in one sentence?
★ have you joined them using a comma or a conjunction?

Examples:

We can link two sentences to:

1. **add another statement** using **and**.

   Jack closed his eyes **and** instantly, he could see the inside of the cave.

2. **add a different option** using **but**.

   He could not see or hear the dragon, **but** he could smell smoke, burning flesh and rotten eggs.

3. **explain the first statement** using **so**.

   Jack knew there was no time to lose, so he started to climb.

Punctuation quests – level 1

Before you move on to the next level, you must complete the table below to confirm that all quests in level 1 have been completed.

	Quests	✓
1.	Ending the period drought in the unit of sense	
2.	BaTtLE oF ThE caPiTaLS	
3.	Interrogation in the Centre of Questions	
4.	The quest for excitement at Shrieking Point!	
5.	The quest for Quotation, the 'God of Speech'	
6.	The search for the attachments of the apostrophes	
7.	The apostrophe myst'ry of the missing letters	
8.	The confusing, bemusing and baffling list comma mystery	
9.	Separated in the comma meaning break	
10.	The, plague of, the comma, splicers	
	Signature: Date:	

MERLIN'S CHALLENGE – LEVEL 1

Correct the errors:

I hope you enjoyed going through the quests. Now is the moment of truth. Hopefully, you have learned a lot about punctuation. I have used the errors in Jack's original draft to set you a challenge. Test your knowledge by completing the challenge, for which I am told a certificate will be awarded.

Punctua has asked me to say that you can always look back at the quests if you are not sure, or even find a knight to ask.

1. **Correct the passage so that it makes sense**

   when jack looked across the cave he could only see shimmering shadows and the shapes of the rocky columns rising out of the gloom he felt for the stone around his neck there was a strange buzzing in the palm of his hand

2. **Spot the comma splicing**

   i. Read the passage aloud.

   ii. Make a mark for each unit of sense.

   iii. Insert a full stop.

      a. Jack slid the leather bundle carefully out of his pouch, and kept a wary eye on the dragon, he unfolded the parcel carefully, if the dragon woke up, now he would be trapped.

      b. There was a sizzle and a crack, quickly Jack pushed his hand into the dragon's mouth, he waited for the fang to drop out.

3. **Capital letters**

   Look for 'I,' names of people, places, days, months and titles and insert a capital letter.

   a. I live in the village of stettle at the foot of spooky summit in the county of north yorkchester.

   b. Merlin and i were due to meet on the first sunday in march.

   c. I have written a book called jack and the crystal fang, and a song, silver hand was written in honour of my triumph.

4. **Question marks – yes or no?**

   Insert either **a question mark** or **a full stop** at the end of these sentences:

   a. Do you feel better now

   b. Jack asked what would happen if he looked away

   c. Jack asked Merlin if he was going with him

   d. Will the dragon wake up while I am trying to get its fang

   e. Jack asked how could he extract the crystal fang

   f. Merlin asked if he was feeling better now

   g. Aren't you coming with me

   h. How can I extract the crystal fang

5. **Exclamation marks**

   When would you use an exclamation mark?

   a.

   b.

   c.

6. **Punctuate the speech (don't forget question marks and exclamation marks)**

   a. Crows' claws I yelled. Do you mean the dragon might wake up.

   b. So many questions Merlin chuckled never fear, Jack. I will be there to guide you.

   c. Merlin turned to Jack and said when you pass through the boulder, you will come to a wall of rock.

   d. Jack Merlin whispered you need to move there isn't much time.

7. **Apostrophes**

   i. Insert the apostrophe in the correct place.

   ii. Check its/it's, their/they're, your/you're.

   a. The pastes' stench made him feel sick and he didnt dare look any closer. Even when he put it into his pouch, it's smell lingered in the air.

   b. Jack didnt know how long hed been standing there with the dragon staring at his silver mark, but all of a sudden, the dragons' nostrils were nearly touching Jacks face. It's huge emerald green eyes looked at Jack's hand.

  c. "Their depending on you Jack. You're they're only hope of finding a cure for the plague. Together, well be able to find the dragon and recover it's fang.

8. Commas in a list

 i. Insert commas to separate the items on the list.

 ii. Explore what would happen if you put the commas in the wrong place.

The paste stunk of blood beetles bats bitter berries body odour and rotten eggs.

9. Identify the people being addressed

Read sentences a, b and c, and discuss questions 1–3 with a partner.

 a. Get the pouch and we can prepare Jack.

 b. It's time. Let's execute Jack.

 c. I've run out of time. I need to wind up Merlin.

 d. "It's your turn to try children," the headteacher shouted.

Questions:

 1. What do these sentences mean?

 2. Where should the comma go?

 3. How does inserting a comma change the meaning?

Tips:

- ★ Read it aloud.
- ★ Does it make sense?
- ★ Start with checking the sentences – mark each unit of words that makes sense.
- ★ It can be a statement, question, exclamation or instruction.
- ★ A sentence always starts with a capital letter and ends with a full stop.
- ★ Commas cannot be used to join two complete sentences.
- ★ To join two sentences, you need to use a conjunction (and, but, so, or).

The fall:

There was a loud crack, Jack looked up, he froze huge chunks of rock tumbled down the mountain one fell onto the path jack dodged out of the way, he slipped, rolled, towards the edge of the path.

Jack held onto a large rock. His fathers dagger. Slipped out of his pocket. He looked, down felt sick. Falcons' Feathers. Where is the village, Jack said, It was a tiny dot far below.

Jack's fingers were frozen it was hard, when he tried to grip the stone. His fingers slipped, he tumbled through the air the air whooshed in his ears.

Part C
Learning punctuation with the characters, level 2

Advanced punctuation to achieve:

★ greater precision.

★ improved flow, impact and effect.

18

Brackets

Quest 1:
Quest for explanations and information in the Land of Brackets

Section 1: Adding extra information

Section 2: Adding explanations

Section 3: Making comments

Section 4: Adding detail and examples

DOI: 10.4324/9781003190509-18

SECTION 1: ADDING EXTRA INFORMATION

> **Brackets: adding extra information**
> ★ Brackets are used to add extra information.

JACK'S RULES:

Brackets can be used to add extra information.

For example:

I wasn't a typical hero (so some people said).

Some said I was shy, weak and a wimp (my story says otherwise).

MERLIN'S MOANS:

If you know about brackets, why didn't you use any in the story? I ended up having to write a Prologue to fill in the gaps. I found them useful in my *Book of Spells* to add extra detail where I thought it would help the writer understand the spell.

PUNCTUA'S POINTS:

Merlin, you should know how important it is to master the basic techniques and rules before you start experimenting with more complicated punctuation.

Brackets add extra information to the writing. For example, in Chapter 1, Jack could have written:

One day, Merlin (**King Arthur's most famous wizard**) returned from the mysterious valleys of South Wales.

Eight years before, Merlin had taken this boy (**Jack**) to live with a family in a village in the north.

This is where our tale begins (**an epic story of the courage of one young boy**).

SECTION 2: ADDING EXPLANATIONS

Brackets

★ Brackets are used to provide additional explanation to help the reader understand what the writer is saying.

JACK'S RULES:

Brackets can be used to add explanations that give extra detail to help the reader understand what the writer is saying.

For example:

Jack opened his pouch and a disgusting stench rose into the air **(cheesy sweat and rotten, fermented eggs)**.

Enormous skeletons and bones covered the floor of the cave **(skulls, arms, legs, ribs, fingers)**.

MERLIN'S MOANS:

I can't say I am a fan. I would have suggested Jack use a colon.

The floor of the cave was covered in enormous skeletons and bones: skulls, arms, legs, ribs, fingers.

PUNCTUA'S POINTS:

As young apprentice writers become more experienced, the next stage is to think about writing to achieve different effects. The choice of punctuation is something for young writers to explore as they experiment with different styles.

For example, you could use a variety of short and more complex sentences and structures. Using brackets to insert short explanations can be extremely effective and add variety to the writing.

For example:

Jack's stomach plummeted (a giant crack had appeared at his feet) and he realised he was trapped on the ledge.

He was shivering uncontrollably (the cold and damp had seeped into his bones).

He trembled as he looked up at Merlin (a truly terrifying figure) towering above him.

SECTION 3: MAKING COMMENTS

JACK'S RULES:

Brackets can be used to add a comment to the reader about what has been written.

For example:

The roast duck I left for the dragon has gone, so it should be asleep soon (**if it worked**).

I'm not sure how long it will last (**hopefully long enough**).

"If you are with me, I will try," Jack said (**if you're not late again**).

MERLIN'S MOANS:

Brackets can be used to make comments (what a great idea!).

Jack Hughes is the author of *The Crystal Fang* (I was the brains behind the project).

PUNCTUA'S POINTS:

Remember: the audience is the reader. The story is a communication between the writer and the reader. Sometimes, for example, the writer wants to whisper some extra information to the reader or add a comment by one of the characters that is not said aloud in the dialogue.

Jack was mocked by the other boys, who thought he was weak, cowardly and useless (golly, would they soon be eating humble pie).

Merlin tried to teach Jack how to punctuate his writing properly, but Jack found it difficult to understand (that's not surprising!).

SECTION 4: ADDING DETAIL AND EXAMPLES

Brackets

★ Brackets can be used to add examples.

★ Commas can be used instead of brackets.

JACK'S RULES:

Brackets can be used to add examples (commas could also be used here).

For example:

He looked for any sign (a gust of cold air, a ray of light) that the entrance was open.

MERLIN'S MOANS:

Brackets can be used to give examples, but I prefer commas myself.

I was disappointed that Jack hadn't tried to think of examples of what I had included in that delicious energy drink to give the reader a clearer idea of what it tasted like (for example, ginger, cinnamon, honey and liquorice).

PUNCTUA'S POINTS:

I do agree with you there, Merlin, but sometimes too much description is unnecessary and slows the story down. It is, however, effective in the right place, for example, using senses other than sight to paint a vivid picture for the reader (such as **sound**, **touch**, **smell** and **taste**).

For example:

Jack leant over to look at the paste, but quickly raised his head because it smelled of something bitter and revolting **(like fermented beetles, boiled bats and bitter berries)**.

Jack knew he was looking for some mark **(for example, a shape carved into the rock)** to show him the location of the entrance.

Jack tried to be as quiet as he could, but every step he took sent a loud noise **(like cracking bones, shattering skulls)** echoing off the walls and down the tunnel.

19

Dashes

Quest 2:
Stress test in the Dash Emphasis Challenge

DOI: 10.4324/9781003190509-19

JACK'S RULES:

Dashes:

★ stress a point.
★ add extra information or an explanation.
★ can be used instead of brackets, a comma or a colon.

For example:

Jack quickly raised his head – **it stunk**.

Jack opened his pouch and a disgusting stench – **cheesy sweat and rotten, fermented eggs** – rose into the air.

Punctua took out some of the punctuation and mixed up other marks in Merlin's Prologue – **that will really wind him up**!

Dashes

Dashes are used to:
★ emphasise a point.
★ add extra information or an explanation.
★ replace brackets.
★ be an alternative to a colon or a comma in a sentence.

MERLIN'S MOANS:

I only like using dashes to stress a point. In his first draft, Jack used them everywhere – what a mess! Thankfully, you removed them before it was published.

Jack could not have written the book on his own – I was the brains behind the project.

I do like a colon or a semi-colon; it is much neater. I would prefer:

Jack quickly raised his head: it stunk.

Jack's heart thudded in his chest; he was on his own.

PUNCTUA'S POINTS:

Merlin, I have told you – again and again – apprentice writers need to develop their own style and experiment with different punctuation marks for effect. Our job is to teach them about the different marks and how to use them. It is their decision which ones they choose. But I do agree that using a variety of marks is important.

Jack looked up at Merlin – **a truly terrifying figure** – towering above him as he wrote.

Merlin's *Book of Spells* was initially missing something – **punctuation**.

Merlin's first sleeping potion recipe – **moths' wings, bats' eyes, gooseberry juice** – was a disaster.

Be warned, punctuation is no joke – **it is dangerous** – any misunderstandings cost lives (for example, Merlin's first draft of the *Book of Spells*).

20

Semicolons

Quest 3:
Quest for connections in the Linking Passages of Semicolons

DOI: 10.4324/9781003190509-20

JACK'S RULES:

Semicolons:

★ link closely related ideas, events and thoughts together.

★ glue two parts of a sentence together that could each work as separate sentences.

★ can be used instead of a **full stop**, **and** or **but**.

There is no capital letter after the semicolon.

For example:

Jack knew he had no time to lose; he started to climb the mountain.

He spun around; a column of fire was tearing down the tunnel towards him.

A pain shot through his leg; his leg buckled under him.

Semicolons

Semicolons are used to:

★ link closely related ideas, events and thoughts.

★ glue two parts of a sentence together that could work as separate sentences.

MERLIN'S MOANS:

I am a *big* fan of semicolons. Using and, and, and, and…can be so boring! Jack has a terrible habit of using **and** when he could use a semicolon.

Merlin likes semicolons; Jack likes the word "and."

Merlin was the brains behind the *Crystal Fang* project; Jack got all the credit.

PUNCTUA'S POINTS:

Semicolons are extremely useful to signal to the reader that the **two sentences are closely linked**. Unlike colons, they must be **preceded by a complete sentence** and **followed by a complete sentence**.

Examples:

Suddenly, the cave fell silent; the crunching had stopped.

Sweat dripped down Jack's forehead and into his eyes; he dared not raise his arm to wipe it away.

Merlin is a famous magician; Jack is a talented writer.

Merlin's spot-free skin recipe was a disaster; it resulted in giant, hairy warts.

21

Colons

Quest 4:
Quest for the list of introductions and explanations in the colon tunnels

DOI: 10.4324/9781003190509-21

JACK'S RULES:

Colons are used to introduce:

★ a list.
★ extra information or an explanation.

They can be:

★ used instead of brackets.
★ a list or a single word.

There is no capital letter after the colon.

For example:

Enormous skeletons and bones covered the floor of the cave: **skulls, arms, legs, ribs, fingers**.

He looked for any sign that the entrance was open: **a gust of cold air, a ray of light**.

Jack had to avoid the dangerous hazards: **the pools of ice at the base of the stalactites, the maze of rocky columns across the cave**.

Colons

Colons are used to:

★ introduce a list.
★ introduce extra information or an explanation.

MERLIN'S MOANS:

I found colons extremely useful in my *Book of Spells*, especially where I needed to give the reader an additional explanation or more information.

Merlin had been the brains behind the *Crystal Fang* project and was miffed: no credit, no acknowledgement, no money!

PUNCTUA'S POINTS:

Colons are extremely useful signals to the reader that an explanation or more information will follow.

Merlin, didn't your first draft of the vanishing spot recipe result in giant hairy warts? Are you sure you used colons to give an additional explanation?

Examples:

Jack shrunk back against the wall**: watched and waited**.

Jack spotted something: **bright jets of red flame and clouds of steam**.

Merlin's *Book of Spells* was initially missing something**: punctuation**.

Be warned punctuation should be treated with great care**: misunderstandings ruin lives**.

Merlin's spot-free skin recipe resulted in giant hairy warts**: a terrible tragedy**.

22

Ellipsis

Quest 5:

Missing in the Land of Ellipses …

DOI: 10.4324/9781003190509-22

JACK'S RULES:

An ellipsis (or ellipses in the plural) is a row of three dots that shows:

★ an interruption – something is missing or still to come.
★ words have been omitted or a sentence has been left unfinished.
★ a speech has been broken off abruptly or paused when someone is thinking.

Remember:

★ a space at both ends.
★ no full stop before an ellipsis even if it comes at the end of a sentence.

For example:

A rush of cold air swirled around Jack and he glanced to his right … Merlin had vanished.

Ellipsis

An ellipsis is a signal that:

★ some words have been left out.
★ a sentence has been left unfinished.
★ dialogue has been interrupted suddenly.

MERLIN'S MOANS:

I think ellipses are used far too often. In my opinion, they should only be considered at a real cliff-hanger as the action comes to a climax and the result is in the balance. For example:

All around him, rock rained from the ceiling. Jack felt dizzy and sick … The thudding was getting nearer and nearer; the ground under him was trembling. Jack didn't move …

PUNCTUA'S POINTS:

An ellipsis, a row of three dots, is also called a suspension or omission mark.

Ellipses are useful to build suspense, for example, by leaving a sentence unfinished at a cliff-hanger. They are also useful for dialogue to indicate:

★ an interruption by another character.
★ that a character is gasping for breath due to his/her exertions.
★ that something has happened or been spotted that has made the character suddenly stop talking.

Examples:

It was silent; the crunching had stopped. Then Jack heard something … swish, swish, swish of a tail across the ground.

As more and more stalactites crashed to the floor, it was becoming harder to see the path to the entrance. Jack had to move. Slowly, he eased himself up. A pain shot through Jack's knee and his leg buckled under him …

The dragon bent closer until its nostrils were nearly touching Jack's face … still Jack did not move … He gripped the stone tighter … willed himself not to look away …

"You chose … the wrong … b … b … boy … sir," Jack stammered.

23
Hyphens

Quest 6:
Quest for meaning in the Land of Hyphen Fasteners

DOI: 10.4324/9781003190509-23

JACK'S RULES:

Hyphens are used to:

★ join two words together to make one new word.
★ make clear what you mean.
★ combine two words to make an adjective.

Hyphens

Hyphens are used to:

★ join two words together.
★ make a meaning clear.
★ combine two words to make an adjective.

For example:

The dragon had **odd-looking** teeth.

Merlin was a very tall, **terrifying-looking** man, with **claw-like** fingernails.

Enormous man eating dragon. (enormous man eating a dragon)

Enormous **man-eating** dragon. (enormous dragon who eats humans)

MERLIN'S MOANS:

I have a great example of a hyphen for you, Punctua.

Punctua has a razor-sharp brain, a tongue to match and an elephant-like memory for any mishaps!

PUNCTUA'S POINTS:

Merlin, weren't you described as a **first-rate** wizard? Maybe, leave writing and teaching to the experts.

Hyphens should be used to **make the writing clear**. Man-eating is a famous example of a possible misunderstanding that could be caused by not using a hyphen. Hyphens are particularly useful to **create new adjectives**.

Examples:

Spot-free rather than a recipe to remove spots.

Fang-like molars is a particular favourite of mine when describing the wicked witch of the north.

24

Bullet points

Quest 7:
Quest for key points at the Bullet Zone

DOI: 10.4324/9781003190509-24

JACK'S RULES:

Bullet points are used to:

★ make brief key points.
★ make the information stand out in list form.
★ help organise information.

For example:

★ Use a full stop after every bullet point that is a complete sentence.
★ Use a full stop after every bullet point that completes the introductory stem.
★ Do not use a full stop after bullet points that are phrases and not complete sentences.
★ Bullet points that are a complete sentence usually start with capitals.

Bullet points

★ are used for brief key points.
★ make a list stand out.
★ set out writing clearly.
★ help to organise information.

MERLIN'S MOANS:

These are a modern invention and weren't around when I wrote my *Book of Spells*. I do like full sentences, but they may have been useful to make my point clearer instead of using colons. For example:

Merlin had been the brains behind the *Crystal Fang* project and was miffed because he had got:

★ no credit.
★ no acknowledgement.
★ no money.

PUNCTUA'S POINTS:

They might have made it easier to read and understand your recipes. For example – "Spot-free skin recipe":

Ingredients:

- ★ a dessertspoon of fermented beetles
- ★ one teaspoon of boiled bats' eyes
- ★ 350ml of gooseberry juice
- ★ half a dozen diced caterpillars
- ★ 100g minced daisy roots
- ★ 100g leech juice

Jack and I have included models in the Appendix for bullet points.

- ★ a job advert for a wizard
- ★ a mission statement for a quest

These will give the apprentice writers a clearer idea of:

- ★ how to use and punctuate bullet points.
- ★ when they are a good tool to use.

Punctuation quests – level 2

Quest 8:

Merlin's challenge check-up for the, plague of the, comma splicers

	WARNING

Some of these quests, challenges and battles may be unsuitable. It is essential that you have been fully trained and are confident in the basic techniques in level 1.

	Quests	✓
1.	Quest for explanations and information in the Land of Brackets	
2.	Stress test in the Dash Emphasis Challenge	
3.	Quest for connections in the Linking Passages of Semicolons	
4.	Quest for the list of introductions and explanations in the Colon Tunnels	
5.	Missing in the Land of Ellipses	
6.	Quest for meaning in the Land of Hyphen Fasteners	
7.	Quest for key points at the Bullet Zone	
8.	Check up for the, plague of, the comma, Splicers	
	Signature: Date:	

MERLIN'S CHALLENGE – LEVEL 2

Check-up for the, plague of the, comma splicers

My punctuation has been changed and needs to be corrected to pass level 2 and earn your Master Editor certificate.

Long, long, ago, when Arthur was King of England there lived a young, boy Jack he became famous throughout the land for his brave and daring deeds, he travelled throughout the country ridding the land of the killer, diseases, sent by the wicked, magician Corona.

When he was young Jack loved listening to stories of knights and wizards, dreamt he would be one of King Arthur's famous knights one day. But there was a problem. Jack wasn't strong, Jack wasn't brave Jack was different from the other boys, in the vIllage, they laughed at him, because, he was useless with a bow and arrow, they made fun of him because he was useless with a sword. They mocked him, because he couldn't run fast, or climb trees, they sniggered at the birth mark on his hand but worse of all for Jack he fainted at the sight of blood.

When Jack was eight years old a Great Plague spread throughout the land, soon the people in Jack's village started getting sick and dying, Jack's mother Ann was covered in huge black boils and so was his father John, they didn't have long to live.

One day a great wizard arrived in the village he was called Merlin and he brought news that there was a cure for the plague.

Appendix

Exploring punctuation: experimenting with style and effect

Use the sections in level 2 and Merlin's Prologue to experiment with:

1. Different types of punctuation. For example:
   ★ brackets, colons, dashes.
   ★ a coordinating conjunction or a semicolon.
2. Changing the sentence structure.
3. Different sentence openers.
4. Different sentence lengths.

PROLOGUE BY MERLIN

Long, long ago, when Arthur was King of England, there lived a young boy, Jack, who became famous throughout the land for his brave and daring deeds. He travelled throughout the country ridding the land of the killer diseases sent by the wicked magician, Corona.

When he was young, Jack loved listening to stories of knights and wizards, and dreamt he would be one of King Arthur's famous knights one day. But there was a problem. Jack wasn't strong. Jack wasn't brave. Jack was different from the other boys in the village. They laughed at him because he was useless with a bow and arrow. They made fun of him because he was useless with a sword. They mocked him because he couldn't run fast or climb trees. They sniggered at the birthmark on his hand. But worse of all for Jack, he fainted at the sight of blood.

When Jack was eight years old, a Great Plague spread throughout the land. Soon the people in Jack's village started getting sick and dying. Jack's mother, Ann, was covered in huge black boils and so was his father, John. They didn't have long to live.

One day, a great wizard arrived in the village. He was called Merlin, and he brought news that there was a cure for the plague.

Wizard wanted urgently

The village of Serpenton urgently needs the assistance of a wizard to rescue it from the plague.

The successful wizard will be able to:

★ grow magic beans.
★ produce a sleeping potion for a dragon.
★ extract a dragon's tooth.

Uniform:

★ a long, bright blue, woollen cloak with bell sleeves and gold trim
★ a matching pointed hat
★ comfortable, ox-hide sandals

Appearance:

★ a very long, white beard and moustache
★ bushy, white eyebrows
★ vivid blue eyes

Personality:

★ brave
★ patient
★ calm

Experience:

★ has lots of experience of dealing with dragons
★ a minimum of three years spellcasting experience

Collect a fang from the King of the Dragons.

When crushed into a powder, a fang from this fearsome dragon can cure the plague that has spread to most of the surrounding villages.

Habitat:

Cave on Dragon's Ridge hidden somewhere on the mountain.

Description:

This enormous dragon has a head bigger than a boulder and eyes that shine like huge emerald balls. It has scales like steel spikes and curved horns that are as sharp as an ice pick. Its long, barbed tail can slash like a whip and tear through the toughest armour with one swipe.

The fang that needs to be taken is as long as a spear and as sharp as a sword.

Completing the mission:

This fearsome fighter has never been defeated by another dragon. The killing of this dragon is strictly forbidden.

The fang can only be collected by putting the King of the Dragons to sleep.

Its favourite food is roast duck. Sprinkling the sleeping potion onto a duck will put the dragon to sleep for long enough to extract the fang.

The fang cannot be removed by any weapon. The only chance of success is to spread a paste of beetle wings, bats' eyes and rowan berries along its gums which will cause the fang to fall out.

GOOD LUCK!

MISSING PERSON REPORT: MODEL

Jack of House Hughes, Serpenton Village.

Jack was last seen two days ago climbing into the mists on Dragon Ridge.

Jack is an eight-year-old and very small for his age. He has emerald green eyes and long, curly blond hair. There is a large birth mark in the shape of a key on his left hand and his two front teeth are missing.

The parents gave the following statement. "We are very worried about Jack. He is a shy and timid little boy and has never left the village of Serpenton before. Anyone who has seen him please get in touch urgently. A search party will be setting out for Dragon Ridge first thing in the morning, and we beg everyone who is well enough to help in the search for Jack."

Planning Template

_____**WANTED URGENTLY**

The village of _____ **urgently need the assistance of a**

_____ **to rescue it from the** _____.

The successful _____ will be able to:

★

★

★

Uniform:

★

★

★

Appearance:

★

★

★

Personality:

★

★

★

Experience:

★

★

QUEST MISSION STATEMENT: TEMPLATE

Planning Template

Collect a _____ **from** _____

_____

_____

_____

can cure _____ that has spread to

most of the surrounding villages.

Habitat:

Description:

Completing the mission

This fearsome fighter has never been defeated _____.

The killing of this _____ is strictly forbidden.

The _____ can only be collected by _____

_____

_____

_____

_____

GOOD LUCK!

MISSING PERSON REPORT: TEMPLATE

Planning Template

MISSING

_____ of _____Village.

_____was last seen _____ago _____

_____.

_____ is an _____ year-old _____ and_____

_____for his age.

He has _____ eyes and _____hair. There is a

_____on his _____.

The parents gave the following statement. "_____

_____

_____

Anyone who has seen him please get in touch urgently. A search party will be setting out for _____first thing in the morning, and we beg everyone _____to help in the search for _____."

As a writer, sometimes you plan the dangerous situations you are going to make your character face, but one of them may literally take you to a dead end. It is, therefore, sometimes necessary to back-track and find another solution.

Your challenge, should you accept it, is to see if you can finish writing the scene below by finding an inventive way of transporting Jack to the top of the mountain to meet Merlin.

Don't forget to try experimenting with some of the advanced punctuation marks for impact and effect.

The storm

Jack struggled to stay on his feet as the wind shoved and tugged fiercely at him. It made it impossible to walk. Jack was sure he would be blown off the path. "Where are you, Merlin? Help me!" Jack yelled.

The thunder roared louder. Then, lightning like a flashing spear lit up the path. Next came the rain. It hammered on his back and stung his face. It was as if he was being blasted by a fire hose and Jack was soaked from head to foot. It was hard to breathe. It was hard to walk, and Jack wasn't sure he would make it, but he kept on climbing.

Suddenly, a loud crack made Jack jump out of his skin. He looked up and froze. An enormous dazzling arrow of lightning lit up the sky. It ripped through the clouds and struck the path in front of him. Jack pressed his back against the side of the mountain and held his breath as a giant crack appeared at his feet. There was nowhere to go. He was trapped. 'Merlin. Help me!' Jack sobbed as the ledge disappeared and Jack tumbled through the air into the dark void below.

What do I do now?' he yelled. Walls of rock surrounded him on all sides. Jack fell to his knees, put his hands to his face and closed his eyes. 'I just want this all to be over. Please, let this nightmare end,' he sobbed, fighting back the tears that were welling in his eyes.

Suddenly, the voice inside his head roared, 'Throw the beans.'

Painfully, Jack rose to his feet. He slid his hand into the wet pouch and felt for the beans. They were wet and slimy and smelt of garlic and sour milk. Thin white strings like worms had sprouted from the tiny split in the middle. Jack wrinkled his nose in disgust and looked around. 'Where shall I throw them? he thought. He turned in a circle and scanned each of the walls. Then, he spotted a hand carved into one of the rocks, so he decided to aim the beans at the hand.

A ball of flashing light spread out like a shimmering rainbow across the wall. Suddenly, the rock began to ripple, and a door appeared. Jack took a deep breath. He slid first one leg and then the other through the doorway and disappeared into the mountain.

Certificate

APPRENTICE EDITOR LEVEL 1

awarded to

Name: _____

In recognition of your hard work in editing your writing.

Jack, Merlin & Punctua _____

_____

Date

Certificate

MASTER EDITOR LEVEL 2

awarded to

Name:

In recognition of your hard work and excellence in mastering the editing process.

Jack, Merlin & Punctua

Date